ETIQUETTE AT HOME

JEANNE NAGLE

rosen publishing's
rosen central

NEW YORK

Published in 2017 by The Rosen Publishing Group, Inc.
29 East 21st Street, New York, NY 10010

First Edition

Library of Congress Cataloging-in-Publication Data

Names: Nagle, Jeanne, author.
Title: Etiquette at home / Jeanne Nagle.
Description: First Edition. | New York City : Rosen Publishing, 2017. | Series: Etiquette rules! | Includes bibliographical references and index.
Identifiers: LCCN 2016029590 | ISBN 9781499464825 (library-bound) | ISBN 9781499464801 (paperback) | ISBN 9781499464818 (6-pack)
Subjects: LCSH: Etiquette for children and teenagers—Juvenile literature.
Classification: LCC BJ1857.C5 N28 2016 | DDC 395.1/22—dc23
LC record available at https://lccn.loc.gov/2016029590

Manufactured in China

CONTENTS

INTRODUCTION

Almost everyone has been told, at one time or another, to mind his or her manners. This is a reminder not to be rude, gross, disrespectful, or thoughtless when around other people. Manners are actually part of a larger guide to polite and civilized living known as etiquette. The two words, "manners" and "etiquette," are often used as if they have the same meaning, but they are not exactly the same. Etiquette is a set, formal way to behave in certain situations. Manners are more general and concern various behaviors themselves. As an example of these two similar terms, consider being the new person in a group. Properly introducing yourself when you meet someone for the first time is considered good etiquette. Not coughing or sneezing into your hand before you shake theirs while being introduced shows you have good manners.

How people learn proper etiquette or attain polished manners varies. Good behavior is often a commonsense thing. If something seems rude or gross to a person, chances are that he or she would not repeat that behavior and risk offending someone else. For adopting the finer points of civilized living, also called the "social graces," there are schools and classes that claim to teach etiquette. Many of these types of lessons apply to students or learners of all ages and may focus on a certain area of etiquette such as dining or business etiquette.

Manners, on the other hand, are first and foremost learned at home. Children and young adults are often at the receiving end of manners lessons and reminders, typically given by someone older—perhaps a parent or grandparent.

Etiquette and manners at home are learned by example and through lessons shared by older family members.

Most people are aware of etiquette and watch their manners when they are in social situations. This is particularly true when they are out in public, or with friends, acquaintances, or even strangers who might judge their behavior. But what about those times when someone is in his or her own home, and the only people around are family members? There are rules of etiquette in this situation as well. However, etiquette at home revolves less around following standard, formal ways of behaving and is more about mutual respect, kindness, and consideration among members of the household.

Modern manners are meant to make others feel comfortable and welcome around each other. That is certainly a goal worth reaching for when one is in a relatively small space, living closely with family members—in other words, at home.

CHAPTER ONE

ETIQUETTE BASICS

Systems or forms of etiquette have existed for millenia. One historical root can be traced back to ancient Egypt, where a man named Ptahhotep wrote a book—actually, a scroll—filled with lessons and suggestions concerning good behavior and human interaction. In seventeenth-century France, etiquette was influenced by how members of the royal court were expected to act, particularly in the presence of the king. Courtesy, which is a component of etiquette defined as polite behavior, has the word "court" in it, revealing its origins. As its practice spread throughout Europe and to the United States, proper etiquette became an even greater symbol of distinguishing the upper class from the lower class.

Today, however, minding one's manners and following socially acceptable rules is more about bringing people together than separating them by category. The definition of proper etiquette has changed through the years, to keep up with social change. Yet some expressions of good manners are timeless; they never go out of style. These may be thought of as etiquette basics.

In sixteenth-century England, Sir Walter Raleigh committed a famous act of courtesy when he supposedly spread his coat over a puddle so the queen's feet stayed dry.

PLEASE AND THANK-YOU

When it comes to manners, saying "please" and "thank-you" is one of the first things you learn. Asking for something and showing appreciation by using polite words is usually the first etiquette lesson people learn.

RESPECTING YOUR ELDERS

In many Asian cultures, elders are shown a great deal of respect in very specific ways. For instance, etiquette in Cambodia dictates that an elder must never be seated lower than a younger person. Cambodians also accept items handed to them by an elder with two hands, never one, while the Chinese make it a point to offer items to an older person using both hands. Cambodians and the Japanese show respect to their elders by bowing when walking by them or greeting them, respectively. In Japan, younger people are supposed to bow lower than their elders do upon meeting, as a sign of respect.

The word "please" is the short version of "if you please," meaning "if you wouldn't mind." British anthropologist David Graeber believes that people frequently make small demands that it would be silly or rude to deny, such as asking someone to pass the salt. Adding "please," he says, makes the demand more civilized, and therefore more polite. Likewise, "thank-you" is also a special term, meant to show that being given something—a present, a kindness, a favor—is welcome and appreciated.

It is tempting not to use "please" and "thank-you" around the house. After all, these seem more like words better used in formal settings, not in the casual atmosphere of one's own home. Some people believe that family members should be

In certain cultures, body language and position, as well as how people interact with each other, are dictated by matters of etiquette.

willing to do nice things for each other without having to be asked politely or thanked afterward. However, a case could be made for saying "please" and "thank-you" to family members mainly because they are the people closest to you, not in spite of it. Others point out that maintaining this etiquette at home will translate to young people, especially, continuing to do so out in public.

WITH ALL DUE RESPECT

Respect involves a sense that someone or something is important and valuable. Family members are the people you are closest to in the world, usually by blood and from living together. For better or worse, your relationship to and with these people makes them important in your life. Treating them with respect makes sense. Respect is reciprocal. This means that if you show someone respect, he or she is more likely to show you respect in return. Therefore, showing respect is not only a civilized way to act, it is also a smart thing to do.

Older people have a lot to teach us, if we only show them respect and the common courtesy of listening to them.

People of all ages should be shown respect as part of proper etiquette. It is especially important to be respectful of the elderly and people who are older than oneself. Not only is it the polite thing to do, but it could be of benefit to you as well. Older people have more experience than younger ones. They have done more, seen more, and accomplished more, mainly because they have been on the planet longer. In the process, they have learned life lessons that they would be happy to share—lessons that could make a younger person's life easier and happier.

NICE ATTITUDE!

Good manners and exceptional behavior are much more effective when they are used within the proper frame of mind. That means being positive and trying to find the good in any situation or person. Behaving in a way that shows consideration for others, which means thinking about someone else's feelings before your own, is a big part of etiquette. Sometimes that can be hard to do. A lot of people find that doing difficult things is made easier by having a positive attitude.

A good attitude also means following etiquette for the right reasons. Behaving well while not really caring about other people is just going through the motions. In a way, it is not being honest—and being honest is an important part of etiquette.

MYTHS AND FACTS

MYTH: It is less important to follow etiquette rules at home than it is to behave well in public.

FACT: Etiquette is about respect, consideration, and making others feel comfortable. These things are especially important in someone's home life, when dealing with the people who are supposed to be closest and dearest to you.

MYTH: Insisting on good manners at home is just another way parents try to control their kids.

FACT: Having good manners is not a matter of control, but rather encouraging self-control. Exhibiting good behavior around the house is a sign of respect and consideration for everyone in the family, including yourself.

MYTH: Etiquette is old-fashioned and does not have any place in today's world.

FACT: While some behavior rules have changed over time, etiquette is just as important and worthwhile as it ever was.

CHAPTER TWO

TABLE MANNERS

Though many people complain that having meals with family may be on the decline, breakfast and dinner together is still a strong tradition and ritual for millions of families. Dining etiquette revolves around seemingly nitpicky things, both for regular family meals and during more formal affairs: which fork to use at different points of the meal, how and where to place a napkin, sorting out how different tableware is used. Most families do not have formal dinners with elaborate place settings when they are eating at home. In that case, it is best to concentrate on table manners instead.

ALL SET

Table manners start even before mealtime itself. Setting the table is an important task. Consider, too, the extra good-manners points earned by offering to set the table in the first place. There is a certain order to how everything is arranged. For purposes of this section, let's say that dinner is the meal being served.

In general, a basic place setting, as a complete dish arrangement is called, is made up of a dinner plate, silverware, a glass for beverages, and a napkin. (Some people use place

A properly set table makes it easier for people to mind their table manners—plus, it looks pretty nice as well.

mats, others do not.) The dinner plate is at the center of the action, and all the other items surround it. The silverware is arranged as if someone were "reading" the place setting, left to right, in order of most common use. The fork goes to the left of the plate, while the knife and spoon are placed to the right, with the knife closer to the plate. The napkin can either be folded once and put underneath the fork or placed on top of the dinner plate.

When setting the table, be sure to leave room in the middle for serving dishes. This area is also where salt, pepper, and other condiments should be placed. Keep in mind that helping to bring food to the table, whether or not you had a hand in cooking it, is another point in one's favor, as is helping to clear the table after the meal is finished.

DINNER IS SERVED

Once food is on the table and everyone is seated, it is time to dig in and get busy eating—or is it? Etiquette requires that

Etiquette and table manners make family mealtimes much more enjoyable, whether it's a simple weekday dinner or a big holiday feast.

every person have food on their plates before anyone takes a bite. Typically, though, that is a rule when dining out or as a guest in someone's home. Many families do not follow this rule in their own homes. Even so, there are still a few maneuvers polite people observe when dinner is first served.

Grabbing greedily at serving plates and taking mounds of food demonstrates bad manners. Instead, take a single portion from the serving dishes nearest you first. Then, if you are feeling generous, you can offer to serve whatever is in those serving dishes to other family members. This is not an absolute must, but merely an extra helping of good manners.

Try not to reach across the table for anything, even if you say "excuse me" while doing so. This motion may block others from either serving themselves or interfere with them eating. You may also knock things over. The polite option is to ask that the desired item be passed to you. Likewise, be ready and willing to pass items to other people.

Finally, taking the last portion of a dish without asking about its availability is rude. Before reaching for that final spoonful of mashed potatoes or the last burger, ask family members if they would like it, or whether they would mind if you finished it.

WATCH YOUR MOUTH

Extreme hunger or the chance to dig into a favorite meal can make even the most polite person forget his or her manners every once in a while. However, shoveling food by the forkful into one's mouth is not polite dinner behavior. The rule of etiquette is that a person takes small bites of food, one at a time, and chews each properly. Such behavior has the extra benefit of helping to keep big gobs of food from getting stuck in your throat when swallowing.

EXCUSE YOU!

Gobbling big bites of food also can lead to swallowing air, which leads to belching. Burping at the dinner table may seem funny, but it is actually very bad manners. Some people have heard that in certain cultures, burping after a meal is considered a compliment to the cook and is expected after a satisfying meal. For most people, however, belching at the table is just plain rude and should be avoided as a matter of etiquette, even at the family dinner table. To a lesser extent, a burp in passing in another context—such as a casual hangout with family at home—is less disruptive than at the table, but still demands an "excuse me." "Pardon me" is also acceptable.

Smaller bites make it easier to keep one's mouth closed while chewing. This brings up another mouth-related rule: do not chew with your mouth open. Food that looks great on a plate looks absolutely awful when it is all ground up from chewing and mixed with saliva. No one wants to see that. Chewing with the mouth closed also makes it easier to chew and eat quietly, another demonstration of good table manners. Talking with your mouth full is also a huge faux pas.

Finally, do not pick your teeth while seated at the table. Excuse yourself to a private area to remove whatever is stuck between your teeth. This is one area in which being at home is an advantage. You can retreat to the bathroom to use a toothpick or dental floss.

There are two things wrong with this picture: 1) The woman is grooming herself in public, and 2) she is using her fingernail instead of dental floss.

BODY LANGUAGE

Etiquette also dictates where and how hands, elbows, and feet should be placed in polite company, including family members at home. One rule lots of people are familiar with is elbows should be kept off the table while people are eating. Experts think that this is a throwback to medieval times, when guests at the royal court were seated close together around a long table. There was not much room to maneuver, and having elbows up on the eating surface took up more space on the eating surface than was practical or allowed. Even though most modern families are not so squashed, there is still a need for personal space while eating, so elbows are still supposed to be off the table.

Several years ago, people were expected to keep their hands folded neatly in their laps when they were not being used to help eat. Nowadays, etiquette does not demand that hands remain frozen in place when not in use. However, they certainly should not be used to play with silverware, drum fingers on the table, or fling pieces of food at brothers and sisters. Likewise, feet should remain flat on the floor as much as possible. Do not kick things or, heaven forbid, prop them up on another chair or the table.

One final piece of advice: do not tip back in your chair at any time during a meal. Not only is it rude, even at home, but you may break the chair legs or hurt yourself in the process.

TEN QUESTIONS TO ASK AN ETIQUETTE EXPERT

1. Which is more important, sticking to etiquette rules or having good manners?

2. When is it OK to interrupt someone during a conversation?

3. Is telling a "little white lie" to save someone's feelings a breach of etiquette?

4. How can I get someone to stop doing something that makes me uncomfortable in my own house?

5. Who should be in charge of making sure I mind my manners at home, me or my parents?

6. How do I politely refuse to eat something I really hate that is being served at dinner?

7. Why do my parents expect me to take my hat off when I'm in the house?

8. What happens when family members have different ideas about how clean is "clean enough"?

9. How do I show respect for my brother/sister when he/she is totally disrespectful toward me?

10. How have the rules of etiquette changed in the past ten/twenty/fifty years?

CHAPTER THREE

LET'S CHAT

Communicating with members of the family or visitors to one's home is not just a matter of chatting at the dinner table or hashing out a problem with someone. Proper etiquette demands that people greet and acknowledge each other. This means saying hello to those present when you enter a room, goodbye when you leave, and taking notice when others say these things to you when they come and go. These rules may seem silly when you live with people, but they are actually a form of good manners.

Most people avoid saying offensive or upsetting things to or in front of their parents and grandparents, aunts and uncles, or other authority figures. Such decorum is easily forgotten with brothers, sisters, cousins, visiting friends—people who are closer to one's own age or younger. In reality, rules of etiquette should apply to everyone you come in contact with, no matter who or how old they are. Everybody slips up following etiquette rules occasionally, but you should avoid making people sad or uncomfortable.

EVERYBODY'S TALKING

Etiquette experts warn people against hogging the conversation. In polite conversation, people take turns talking.

In a group setting, even with family, everyone should take turns talking. Also, young people show respect by letting older people finish their thoughts before interrupting.

Everyone gets a chance to express himself or herself. That is why you should let your younger siblings tell you the latest joke they heard, even if it is not very funny, or weigh in about where they think the family should go on vacation. If your parents had a hard day at work, let them share a story or two at the dinner table. It is bad manners to interrupt someone when it is his or her turn to speak.

When it is your time to speak, whenever possible, think through what you want to say before you say it. You are less likely to blurt out something hurtful, rude, or inaccurate.

Etiquette experts used to recommend that people prepare for conversations with a list of topics. You need not go that far, especially not at home. But you might want to have a conversation starter in your communications toolbox, just in case there is a lengthy pause in conversation. Keeping conversation interesting is a good social skill.

It also is polite to include everyone when having a group conversation. If several family members or a group of friends are in the same room talking, do not spend all your time chatting with only the sibling closest to you or your best friend. Making someone feel left out of the conversation is rude.

Communication is not just talking, but also listening. The latter requires being attentive. By paying attention and giving some thought to what others are saying, you are able to respond with similar or related thoughts and ask meaningful questions.

WHAT YOU SAY

Being tactful includes minding what you say, beyond simple word choice and paying compliments. What you say should be as truthful as possible, without gossiping. Proper etiquette requires that you try to build up others' confidence, not tear them down.

Modern-day etiquette experts often add honesty to their list of qualities, alongside respect and consideration. You are less likely to lie to someone you respect. Most parents expect and require that their children and other family members are honest. Honesty should not be used merely as a license to say something nasty to someone, however. Well-mannered people do not intentionally hurt people's feelings.

ATTENTION, PLEASE

People have come to rely on all sorts of portable electronic devices, particularly cell phones and smartphones, for communication, information, and entertainment. It is common now to see a group of friends or family members in the same place but all looking at their screens, their fingers swiping or tapping out messages. Checking texts and following social media posts when you are supposedly talking with other people can become a habit—one that

(continued on the next page)

Etiquette requires that people pay more attention to whoever is sitting next to them than to whoever, or whatever, is reachable by phone.

(continued from the previous page)

needs to be broken, according to etiquette experts.

When you are with other people, hanging out or having a conversation, it is rude to ignore them in favor of your cell phone. That means no checking your Twitter or Facebook account "for just a second," making or receiving calls, or texting. Doing so is the same thing as if you walked away in the middle of someone who was talking. If you absolutely have to take a call or contact someone immediately, excuse yourself and leave the person or group you are with before doing so. Leave all social media stuff for later, when you are not being social in person.

Gossip may be false or exaggerated information, but even if it is true, it is no reason to share stories that are not yours to share in the first place. Those who have good manners do not talk about others behind their backs. Gossip is not appropriate behavior, even when it happens between family members concerning the actions of someone else in the household.

Many brothers and sisters like to pick on each other, and when caught by their parents they cry, "I was only teasing!" Such a defense is merely an attempt to disguise bad manners. Teasing and mocking upset the intended target. They are just as unacceptable at home as they are anywhere else.

HOW YOU SAY IT

How one says something is often just as important as what is being said. "Tone" is the term used to describe how something sounds, and the feelings that sound stirs inside the

"I SWEAR!"

Swearing is using rough or inappropriate language, usually when angry. Throughout the ages, swear, or curse, words have been considered "common" language, meaning language used by lower-class or unrefined persons. In the past, the habits—including the language—of the lower classes were considered to be lacking etiquette. Swearing therefore became associated with bad manners.

Of course, cursing is an etiquette trouble spot for people of all social backgrounds. Curse words are considered offensive and therefore are never used in "polite" conversation. If the object of etiquette is to make people comfortable and not to offend anyone, then swearing would be a show of bad manners. Many parents frown on swearing or forbid it altogether. Hence, it is best to avoid it as a sign of respect to one's parents and household, and its rules, as well as within a framework of proper etiquette.

people who hear it. To understand this concept, think about someone asking for something angrily, but saying, "Please!" Technically, the person asking is showing good manners, but his or her aggressive and demanding tone ruins it. Whining is also another thing most people find annoying. Avoid it whenever possible.

Volume also makes a difference when speaking. Good manners dictate that yelling is only appropriate when someone

Yelling, waving one's hands, and making faces while talking are definitely not signs of a proper—or even useful—conversation with family members.

is too far away to be heard at a respectful volume. Even then, increasing the volume of one's voice can be unsettling. The opposite, being too quiet, also can cause problems, with people straining to hear. At home, children often speak very softly, so-called under their breath, when they want to say something disrespectful to their parents but they don't want to get punished for saying it. Etiquette experts strongly suggest that people speak in a pleasant tone, at an appropriate volume.

CHAPTER FOUR

CLEANLINESS AND APPEARANCE

An old saying declares, "Cleanliness is next to godliness." In other words, being clean is a virtue, a sign of good behavior. Keeping clean and making sure your living space is tidy are other expressions of good manners.

Cleanliness is not simply bathing or washing regularly, or picking up a pile of worn clothes from the bedroom floor. Etiquette takes into account the way a person looks overall. Clothing, accessories, hairstyle, grooming, and more all affect a person's appearance.

NEAT AND TIDY

Houses and apartments are shared spaces. People living together sometimes have very different ideas about what constitutes acceptable living conditions. Typically, young children and teenagers don't mind their stuff being all over the place, whereas adults like a bit more order. Even if your parents are very relaxed about neatness, it is good etiquette to keep your living space in at least relatively neat order. Cleanliness shows that you care, not only about how your

Some people think they have the right to live in a messy room, but etiquette means that everyone's feelings should be taken into consideration in such matters.

home appears but also about the people you live with. Forcing them to deal with your mess is a big breach of etiquette.

Any room that belongs mostly or completely to one person is the responsibility of that person. Therefore, every person should take care of his or her own bedroom. Each person living in a home should do his or her part to keep common areas clean, such as the living room and the kitchen. One simple rule to follow is if you make or help make a mess in a common area, you are responsible for cleaning it up.

GOOD GROOMING

Keeping oneself clean is perhaps even more vital than one's living spaces. There are several reasons why taking a shower, brushing your hair, etc., have become part of most people's daily routine. Washing and grooming shows that a person has consideration for others and respects themself, too.

Obviously, bathing should be done in private. However, proper etiquette holds that most, if not all, personal grooming should be done away from the public eye as well. Grooming

Performing chores that help keep a home clean and organized, such as doing the family laundry, is proper etiquette.

Shaving is a grooming ritual that good manners dictate should be done in private. Cleaning the sink out afterward also is a polite move.

involves a lot of applying, treating, cleaning, and removing things that are best not shared with others. Even something as simple as brushing one's hair can be a problem, because loose strands and/or dead skin cells (dandruff) can land on a housemate or his or her possessions. In addition to hair brushing, grooming habits that should be done in the privacy of one's own room or bathroom include:

Applying—deodorant, lotion, perfume, nail polish

Removing—toenails and fingernails (by trimming or filing), calluses or scabs, or pimples

Treating/cleaning—cleaning ears, brushing teeth, flossing

IT'S A WASH

Washing up isn't only something you should do in the shower or before dinner. Imagine that you are trying to watch your favorite show on television in the family living room. In strolls your brother, who has just come from a three-mile (five-kilometer) run. Sweat is making his shirt stick to him, and his legs are splattered with stinky mud. He likes the show, too, and plunks himself down right next to you. As if his armpit BO (body order) isn't bad enough, he kicks off his shoes, so you

NOSES UNDERCOVER

There are several etiquette rules that concern things going into or coming out of a person's body. One of the most well known of these is that polite people cover their noses when they sneeze. At the very least, one should do so into one's sleeve or clothes if sneezing into one's hands is problematic. Avoid sneezing right on a family member, out into the air, or on furniture or common surfaces. This simple maneuver helps stop a spray of germs from covering anyone in the area. Blowing your nose also has a rule attached to it that many people often break without thinking about it: that a person should not check to see what is inside the tissue after blowing.

In the United States, it is considered polite to say, "God bless you," "Bless you," or "Gesundheit!" when someone sneezes. This phrase is said to have arisen in the fourteenth century, when Europe suffered a plague pandemic. People hoped the ones who sneezed were not becoming deathly ill. Hence, their well wishing was a sort of mini-prayer that became a ritual or tradition over time.

If you observe someone sneezing or having some trouble with a stuffed-up nose, and you have access to facial tissues or napkins, it is customary to offer some to the person.

get that aroma as well. Gross, right? More than that, it shows disrespect for others in the room—namely you and your nose—and is, therefore, very bad manners.

Unless you live in a bubble, dirty and germy things are going to happen to you from time to time. The key is to handle such situations like an etiquette professional by making things neat, clean, and tidy again using a little soap and water.

COMFORTABLE VS. THOUGHTFUL

In olden times, upper class people used to dress up in their finest formal clothing merely to share a family meal. Few modern adults, teenagers, or children come to breakfast or dinner wearing a tuxedo/suit or gown/dress. However, you should still make an effort to look presentable when spending time with family at home, if only for etiquette's sake. This means not wearing ratty clothes or outfits that might be considered a little too revealing. Running a quick comb through your hair, even if you're just going to watch TV with your family, is another nice way to show consideration.

Some people would argue that they should be comfortable in their own homes and not worry about how they look. The response by some may be "fair enough," but that is no reason to be a total slob. Keeping up your appearance is not only good manners, it also shows you respect yourself as well.

CHAPTER FIVE

SPACE AND TIME

The rules of etiquette extend to such abstract concepts as space and time. Areas of concern here include privacy, minding your own business, and being on time.

PRIVACY, PLEASE!

Many people try to strike a balance between privacy or alone time and socializing. People do not have to be hiding

Some people use alone time for hobbies, such as jewelry making. Family members need to respect each other's privacy, no matter why it is desired.

35

DIGITAL PRIVACY

These days, people frequently use computers and other electronic devices to communicate. Households sometimes have shared computers or other electronic devices. In other households, everyone has their own devices. Proper etiquette states that digital communications remain private, even if they are sent or kept on a shared computer or device. Using someone else's computer or other electronic device is a huge no-no, unless two or more users have an understanding.

This situation gets a bit tricky when parents attempt to monitor their children's home internet use, particularly their presence on social networking platforms and applications. In order to help keep kids safe, parents may bend privacy etiquette rules by checking their children's email and accounts or otherwise surveying their usage. They may download software that lets them filter or even block certain sites on the family computer or the child's cell phone. Is this merely a case of parental bad manners or an extreme invasion of privacy? The opposite seems true only rarely—that is, children seldom are very interested in their parents' digital lives. It truly depends on what boundaries each family has constructed internally and what expectations children and siblings have. People have widely varying opinions on this subject, and each family unit will have different standards. In many families, the differences of opinion on this very topic can be a serious bone of contention. Ultimately, each family must choose its own stance regarding online privacy.

something or keeping a secret to want a little privacy. This can mean having actual, physical space to oneself for a length of time or wanting to keep one's possessions and property out of others' hands and away from prying eyes. Privacy gives people time to think and be themselves, and lets them recharge.

A closed door usually signals that the person inside wants to be left alone. Always knock and listen for verbal permission to enter before doing so. Someone might be asleep or otherwise busy. If you know they may be preoccupied and have headphones or music on, you might try knocking a little harder. Otherwise, it is better to knock more discreetly and then try again later if no one answers.

CLAIMING TERRITORY

Humans can be quite territorial by nature, even in their own homes. Claiming a favorite spot on the sofa or preferring to sit in a special chair at the kitchen table are all common behaviors. If someone's preference for a particular seat or location is known, then it would be good manners to make every attempt possible to honor that preference. In other words, do not take over someone's spot merely because you can or to get a rise out of them.

Some locations at home are a single person's territory because that is where that person chooses, or has been assigned, to spend most of his or her time. The best example of this is a person's bedroom. In the case of shared bedrooms, a person's territory is generally a specific side of the room or an unmarked but implied area surrounding his or her bed and things.

Disagreements with family members over space and possessions are bound to happen. But staying calm and respecting each other can work wonders.

YOURS AND MINE

People are territorial over space and also over their possessions. In each household, there are items that belong to the household members collectively and those that are the property of a specific individual. Good manners come into play mainly when there is a disagreement about how to best take turns with the shared items. Personal possessions, however, are always covered by the rules of etiquette.

If something belongs to another family member, the general rule is to keep your hands off of it. This applies even if there is an item that used to belong to you, but it has been given to someone else, such as clothing, a book, or a computer game. Asking the owner, or new owner, to borrow an item is the polite and correct thing to do. Once you have borrowed something, remember these two simple rules: do not keep it for longer than you need it and always return what you borrow in as good or better condition than it was in when you took temporary possession. While better may be impossible with a book or similar item, you can always borrow something and clean or fix it as an extra repayment of the favor your family member did for you.

BEING ON TIME IS NOT RELATIVE

Arriving and being ready on time is called punctuality. In general etiquette terms, punctuality is important because it is rude to keep other people waiting. The same is true when it comes to etiquette at home, but there is also another dimension to being on time with family. Missing curfew and not coming home after school as you said you would also tend to get you in trouble with your parents, in addition to being disrespectful.

It may seem that a meal at home—especially if you are already home, but perhaps upstairs or outside—does not require as much punctuality as a dinner date elsewhere. But etiquette demands that you make it on time to the table. After all, if others are abiding by proper etiquette, they will not start without you, and delaying them is selfish. It is also rude to those who prepared the meal and helped set the table. Even if you're not asked, show up with enough time to offer your assistance.

If you are out and about, try your best make it home on time. If your plans change, or you know you are going to be late, be sure to call or text the person who is waiting for you. It is especially important to let your parents know where you are and when you'll be home.

HOME AWAY FROM HOME

Some people believe that etiquette at home matters only inside their own house. They think that when they are on vacation or visiting relatives for the holidays, they can take a break, or at least lighten up a little, on the good manners. Unfortunately for them, the same rules of etiquette that people follow at home apply when they are in a homelike setting somewhere else. A hotel room is basically the same as sharing a bedroom, and a relative's home is like an extension of your own home. The location may change, but the dynamic—the way people behave in a certain situation—does not and should not.

Practicing good manners at home is just that—practice. Brushing up on your etiquette in the comfort and relative safety of your own house is excellent preparation for those times when manners are required in social and business situations, now and in the future. As is the case with so many life lessons, all the best etiquette training begins at home.

GLOSSARY

abstract Having to do with general ideas rather than concrete items or actions.

acknowledge To admit that something is true or exists.

appropriate Something that is right or suited to a particular situation.

attentive To think about something or pay careful attention to it.

breach To break a promise, rule, or law or neglect one's duty.

civilized Being polite, reasonable, and respectful, usually by following a set of rules that concern how people treat each other.

condiments Seasonings and sauces that give food extra flavor.

consideration A desire to avoid doing something that will offend or hurt someone.

etiquette A set of rules that help guide people toward good behavior and manners.

extended Going beyond the usual or basic version of something.

filter To select for removal.

maneuver To move carefully and skillfully.

preference Wanting or liking something over other similar items.

prying Trying to find out information about private matters.

reciprocal When two parties agree to treat each other in a similar way, so that both benefit.

respect A feeling that someone or something is worthy of being treated well and kindly.

territorial Protecting an area that one feels is special to him or her.

timeless Staying important or fashionable over time; lasting forever

virtue Having good character and behaving well.

FOR MORE INFORMATION

The American Civility Association
One Independent Drive, Suite 102
Jacksonville FL 32202
(904) 612-5031
Website: http://americancivility.org
The American Civility Association is a nonprofit group that seeks to
educate children and families about civility and the far-reaching
consequences of not being respectful and considerate. The group
provides civility awareness training and educational materials
geared primarily toward children, grades pre-K through twelve.

The Canadian School of Protocol and Etiquette
380 Wellington Street, 6th Floor
London, ON N6A 5B5
Canada
(519) 964-5725
Website: http://thecanadianschoolofprotocol.com
The Canadian School of Protocol and Etiquette provides guidance
with regard to etiquette, protocol, and civility—all with a
decidedly Canadian bent. The school offers group seminars,
private coaching, and online resources.

Civility Experts Worldwide, Inc.
192 Tache Avenue
Winnipeg, MB R2H 1Z6
Canada
(204) 966-4792
Website: http://www.civilityexperts.com
Based in Winnipeg, Civility Experts Worldwide offers civility training,
certification, workshops, and webinars. The organization also
serves as a resource for materials concerning civility and etiquette.

The Emily Post Institute, Inc.
444 South Union Street

Burlington, VT 05401
(802) 860-1814
Website: http://emilypost.com
This family business is staffed by descendants of world-renowned
    etiquette expert Emily Post. The institute publishes books and
    articles on etiquette and manners, and also conducts seminars
    and training on the same subjects.

Girls Rule!
PO Box 305
Oak Park, IL 60303
(312) 479-0789
Website: http://girlz-rule.org
The mission of Girls Rule! is to empower young women in urban
    areas through several programs, including etiquette training.

The National School of Etiquette and Protocol
The Crescent Center
400 Crescent Court, Suite 400
Dallas, TX 75201
(972) 804-8848
Website: http://www.nationalschoolofetiquette.com
The National School of Etiquette and Protocol offers seminars and
    training. The organization offers workshops and activities geared
    toward particular groups, including youth.

WEBSITES

Because of the changing nature of internet links, Rosen
Publishing has developed an online list of websites related to
the subject of this book. This site is updated regularly. Please
use this link to access the list:

http://www.rosenlinks.com/ER/home

FOR FURTHER READING

Barnes, Emilie. *Good Manners in Minutes: Quick Tips for Every Occasion.* Wheaton, IL: Tyndale House Publishers, 2010.

Browne, Kelly. *101 Ways to Say Thank You: Notes of Gratitude for All Occasions.* New York, NY: Sterling, 2015.

Diamond, Susan. *Social Rules for Kids: The Top 100 Social Rules Kids Need to Succeed.* Shawnee Mission, KS: AAPC Publishing, 2011.

Eberly, Sheryl. *365 Manners Kids Should Know: Games, Activities, and Other Fun Ways to Help Children and Teens Learn Etiquette.* New York, NY: Three Rivers Press, 2011.

Eding, June. *Manners That Matter Most: The Easy Guide to Etiquette at Home and in the World.* Hobart, NY: Hatherleigh Press, 2014.

Felix, Rebecca. *Good Manners with Your Parents.* Minneapolis, MN: Magic Wagon, 2014.

Felix, Rebecca. *Good Manners with Your Siblings.* Minneapolis, MN: Magic Wagon, 2014.

Furgang, Kathy. *Netiquette: A Student's Guide to Digital Etiquette.* New York, NY: Rosen Publishing Group, 2011.

Martin, Judith. *Miss Manners' Guide to Domestic Tranquility: The Authoritative Manual for Every Civilized Household, However Harried.* Danvers, MA: Crown Publishing 2011.

Packer, Alex J. *How Rude! The Teen Guide to Good Manners, Proper Behavior, and Not Grossing People Out.* Minneapolis, MN: Free Spirit Publishing, 2014.

Post, Peggy, et al. *Emily Post's Etiquette 18th ed.: Manners for a New World.* New York, NY: HarperCollins Publishers, 2011.

Scott, Jennifer. *Polish Your Poise with Madame Chic: Lessons in Everyday Elegance.* New York, NY: Simon & Schuster, 2015.

Smith, Jodi R. R. *The Etiquette Book: A Complete Guide to Modern Manners.* New York, NY: Sterling Publishing, 2011.

Woodfine, David. *ABCs of Etiquette for Young People.* Franklin, TN: Hilliard Press, 2015.

BIBLIOGRAPHY

Ashgar, Rob. "27 Etiquette Rules for Our Times." *Forbes*, April 22, 2014 (http://www.forbes.com/sites/robasghar/2014/04/22/27-etiquette-rules-for-our-times/#451c951f61dc).

Culinarylore.com. "No Elbows on the Table?" November 2012 (http://www.culinarylore.com/food-history:no-elbows-on-the-table).

The Emily Post Institute. "Good Grooming and Wardrobe Care," 2016 (http://emilypost.com/advice/good-grooming-and-wardrobe-care).

English, Suzanne-Marie. *The Etiquette of Kindness: It's Not Just About the Right Fork.* Rescue, CA: Pleasant Ranch Publishing, 2012.

Factsanddetails.com. "Chinese Customs, Manners, and Etiquette," June 2015 (http://factsanddetails.com/china/cat4/sub19/item114.html).

Forni, P. M. *Choosing Civility: The Twenty-Five Rules of Considerate Conduct.* New York, NY: St. Martin's Press, 2002.

McKay, Brett, and Kate McKay. "The Art of Conversation: 5 Dos and Don'ts." The Art of Manliness, September 24, 2010 (http://www.artofmanliness.com/2010/09/24/the-art-of-conversation).

Mony, Keo. "General Etiquette in Cambodian Society." EthnoMed.com, January 2004 (http://ethnomed.org/culture/cambodian/general-etiquette-in-cambodian-society#section-4).

Nova Online. "Einstein's Big Idea," June 2005 (http://www.pbs.org/wgbh/nova/einstein/hotsciencetwin).

Oliver, Dana. "Nail Clipping, Flossing Teeth, and 13 More Personal Grooming Habits That Should Never Be Done In Public." Huffingtonpost.com, November 15, 2012 (http://www.huffingtonpost.com/2012/11/15/nail-clipping-flossing-teeth-personal-grooming_n_2133867.html).

Packer, Alex J. *How Rude! The Teen Guide to Good Manners, Proper Behavior, and Not Grossing People Out.* Minneapolis, MN: Free Spirit Publishing, 2014.

Popova, Maria. "How We Got 'Please' and 'Thank You': Why the Line Between Politeness and Bossiness is a Linguistic Mirage." Brainpickings.com, July 25, 2013 (https://www.brainpickings.org/2013/07/25/origin-of-please-and-thank-you).

Reuters. "The Dos and Don'ts of Cell Phone Etiquette." *New York Daily News*, July 23, 2013 (http://www.nydailynews.com/lifestyle/good-mobile-manners-article-1.1406873).

Tasteofhome.com. "How to Set a Table," 2016 (http://www.tasteofhome.com/recipes/how-to-cook/how-to-set-a-table).

Toksvig, Sandi. *The Tricky Art of Co-Existing: How to Behave Decently No Matter What Life Throws Your Way.* New York, NY: The Experiment, LLC, 2015.

Walters, Marla. "10 Rules of Etiquette That Everyone Should Know (and Follow)." Wisebread.com, December 2013 (http://www.wisebread.com/10-rules-of-etiquette-everyone-should-know-and-follow).

Wikiel, Yolanda, and Kaitlyn Pirie. "Proper Etiquette for Every Occasion." Realsimple.com, 2014 (http://www.realsimple.com/work-life/work-life-etiquette/proper-etiquette).

INDEX

ABOUT THE AUTHOR

Jeanne Nagle has been practicing good manners for so many years she is now an elder who deserves respect. She has supplemented such experiential learning with thorough research in the creation of this book.

PHOTO CREDITS

Cover, pp. 7, 14, 22, 29, 35 (top) Africa Studio/Shutterstock.com; cover (bottom) Hero Images/Getty Images; p. 5 Robert Nicholas/OJO Images/Getty Images; p. 8 Bob Thomas/Popperfoto/Getty Images; p. 10 Randy Faris/Corbis/VCG/Getty Images; p. 11 Thinkstock/Stockbyte/Getty Images; p. 15 bradleym/ E+/Getty Images; p. 16 Chuck Savage/Corbis/Getty Images; p. 19 Judith Haeusler/Cultura/Getty Images; p. 23 Klaus Vedfelt/Taxi/Getty Images; p. 25, 31 JGI/Jamie Grill/Blend Images/Getty Images; p. 28 SW Productions/Photodisc/Getty Images; p. 30 Photofusion/Universal Images Group/Getty Images; p. 32 PaoloBis/Moment Open/Getty Images; p. 35 Hero Images/Getty Images; p. 38 Universal Images Group/Getty Images.

Designer: Michael Moy; Editor: Philip Wolny;
Photo Researcher: Philip Wolny